is for Britain

Tear and Share Colouring Book

Quality Perforated Pages A – Z • Educational Family Fun

Helen Ashley

D1824022

www.colourmeart.com

Printed in Britain

ISBN 978-0-9871854-2-6

Illustrated by Helen Ashley .
First published by ColourMeArt™, 2012
P.O Box 777, Petersham, NSW , Australia 2049.

For more of Helen's original ideas visit
www.colourmeart.com or helenashleydesigns.com

HELEN ✾ ASHLEY

All **ColourMeArt**™ products are hand-drawn and painted by Helen Ashley.

With a degree in Textile Design and Art History from Loughborough College
of Art, Helen has sold her artwork worldwide and has designed for fashion,
bed-linen, swimwear, children's wear , ceramic homewares, and stationery.
She has also illustrated several other books apart from this one.

According to her mum, Helen showed her love of colour and pattern with peals
of laughter from just three weeks old! Helen has created the **ColourMeArt**™
range to encourage an early love of colour and screen-free creativity for
both boys and girls.

Helen lives with her husband and three children in Sydney, Australia.

CONTENTS

A

King Arthur
Avebury Stone Circle
Adder

B is For Britain

B

B

B is for Britain

Bus

Black cab

Beefeater

Big Ben

The Beatles

www.colourmeart.com

C

C

Coronation Crown

D

D

Devonshire Cream Tea
Dartmouth Castle
The River Dart
Sir Francis Drake's Ship

www.colourmeart.com

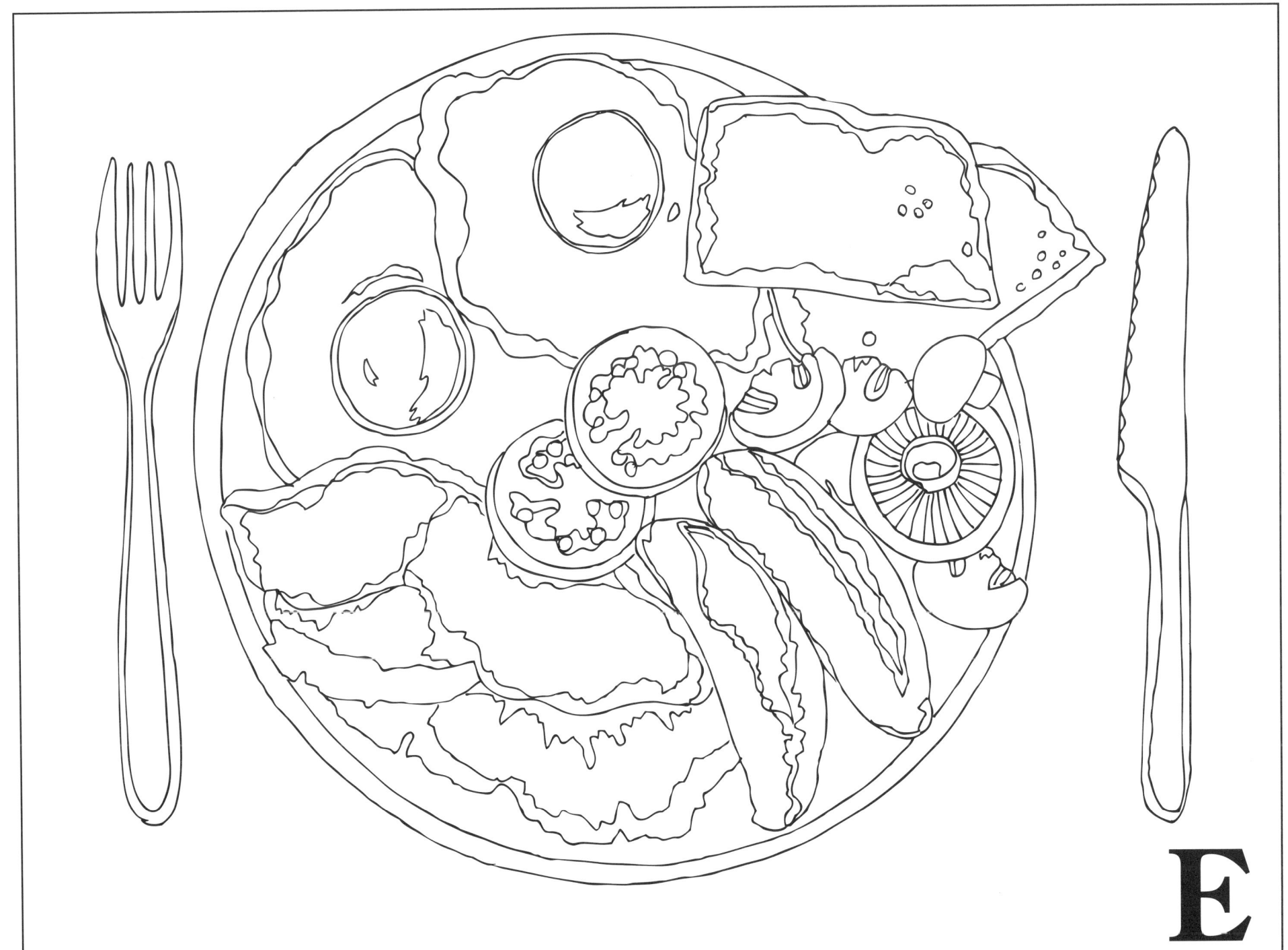

E

E

English Breakfast

Eggs and bacon

www.colourmeart.com

F

F

Football
Fox

G

G

Garden

Green Wellies

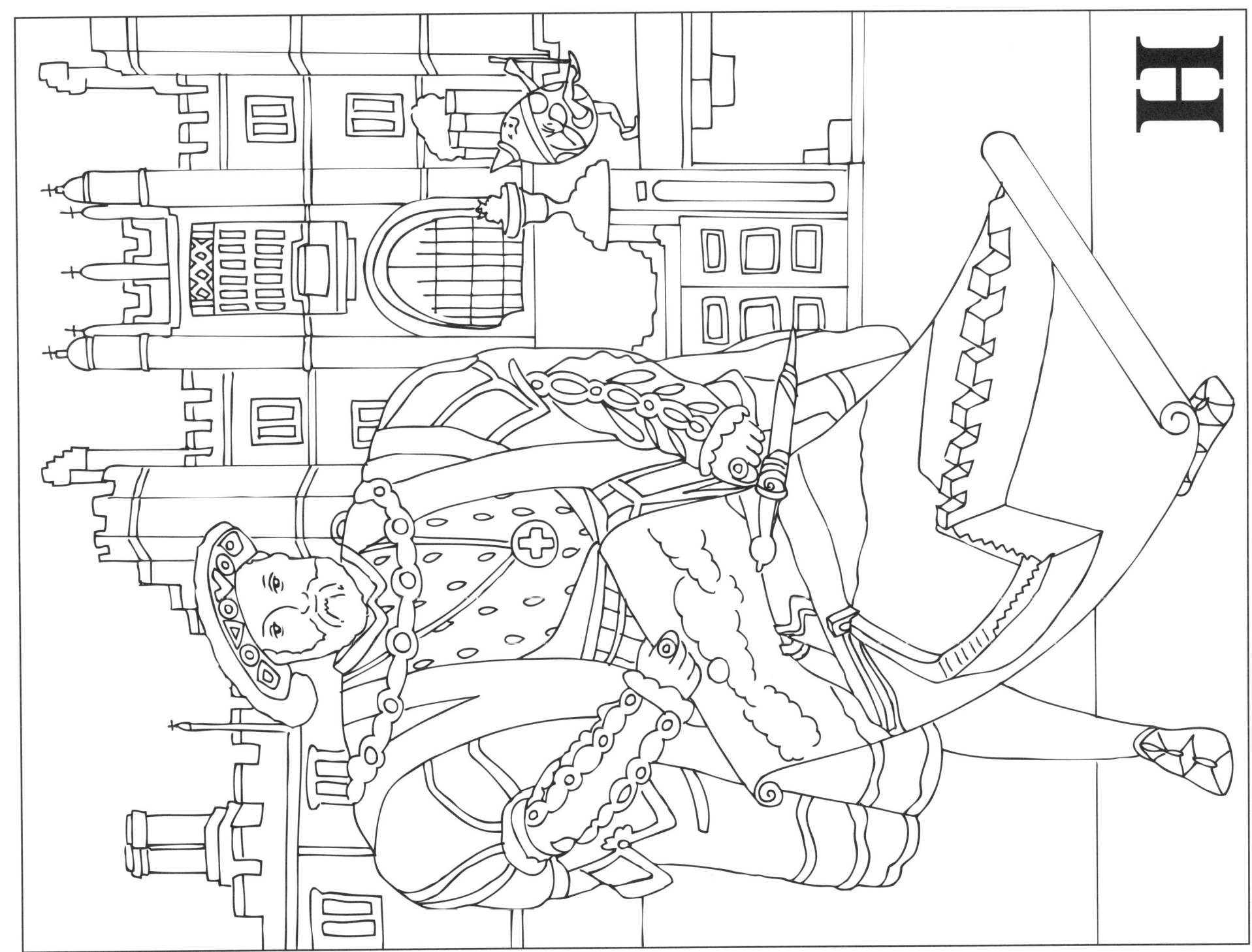

H

Henry VIII
Hampton Court
Hadrian's Wall
Humpty Dumpty

www.colourmeart.com

I

Industrial Revolution

Iron Bridge 1779

J

Jester Jolyon juggling

Jaffa Cakes

Jammy Dodgers

Jimmy's Jellied Eels

www.colourmeart.com

K

K

Jousting Knights

L

Landowner Lawrence eats Lardy cake.

Land Rover

Loch Ness Monster

www.colourmeart.com

M

M

Marmalade on toast

Mug of tea

www.colourmeart.com

N

Notting Hill Carnival

www.colourmeart.com

O

O

Owl

Oxo cube

Os and Xs

Otter

Oxo building

www.colourmeart.com

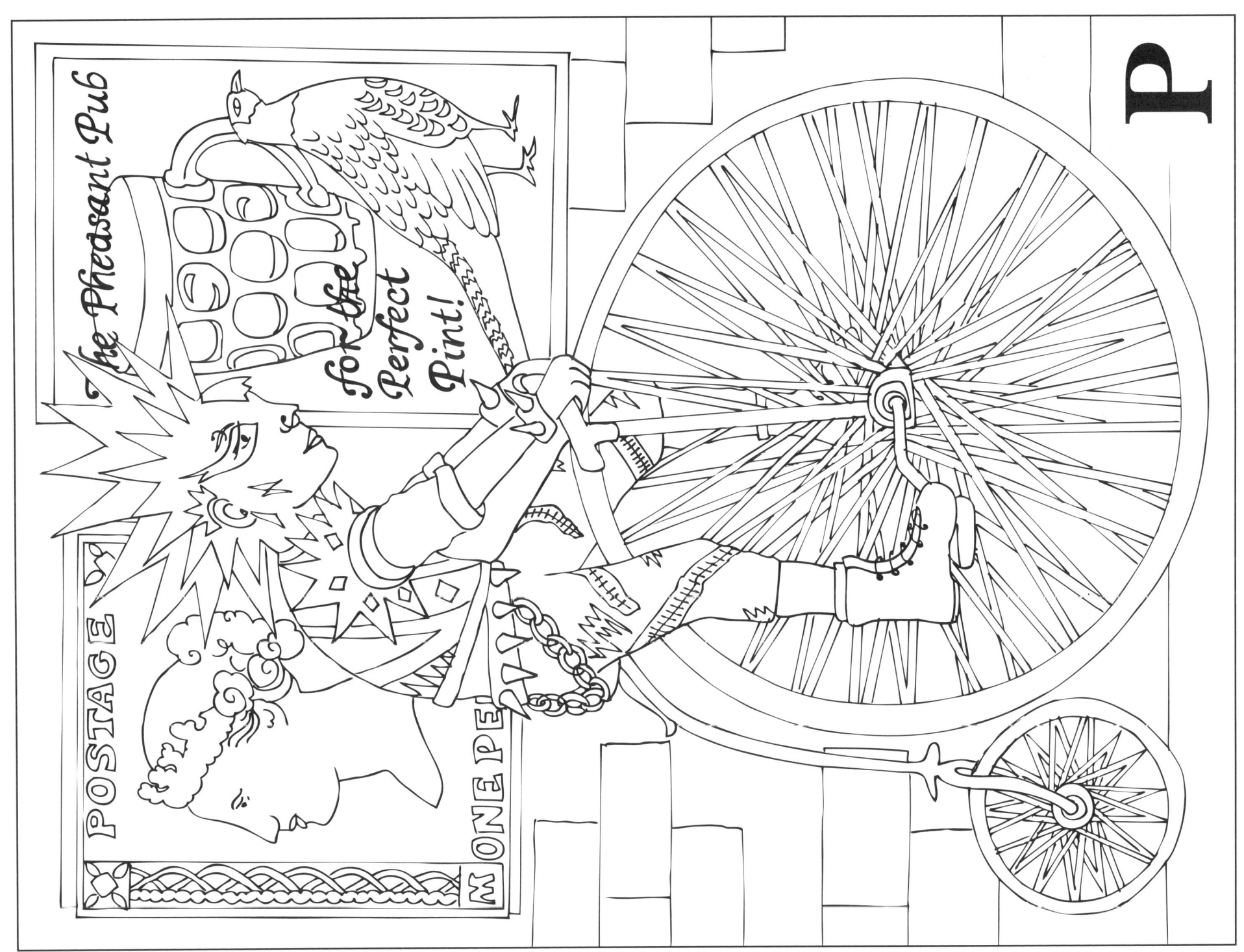

P

Pete the Punk
Penny Farthing
Penny Black Postage Stamp
Pheasant Pub
Pint of Beer.

Q

Q

Queen Elizabeth I

R

R

Robin Hood

Royal Messenger

Rochester Castle

Regal rose

A Robin Redbreast

Red Radishes

www.colourmeart.com

S

S

Squirrels

Stonehenge

Summer pudding

Strawberries and Cream

Shakespeare's Sonnets

Swan

www.colourmeart.com

T

Tommy the Tourist

Thames Tour

The Tower of London

Tower Bridge

Tartan hat

Thistle Tattoo

Mrs Tiggy Winkle

Telephone

Tin of Twinings Tea

The Times

Titanic

Thatched Cottage

www.colourmeart.com

U

Unicorn
Uffington White Horse
Underground
United Kingdom
Union Jack

V

Queen Victoria

V and A museum logo

Victoria Sponge Cake for V E Day

Victory flags

W

W

Welsh Dragon with Welsh flag
Welsh hills

www.colourmeart.com

X

The Royal Kiss

www.colourmeart.com

Y

Yorkshire Terrier
York Rose
York Minster
Yorkshire puddings

Z

Z

ZZZZZ-

Bees Buzzing

Zac's Dad znoozzing

www.colourmeart.com